Cover design by:
Salem Alliance Church Graphic Department
Jeff Brown
Materials created by:
Salem Alliance Church Bible Study Department
Barbara Fletcher, Sarah Morrow, Susan Garlinger, Kyle Dalen, Cary Wood
Published 2017
Printed by permission only

CONTENTS

PREFACE

To many people the word *ridiculous* conjures thoughts like "absurd, silly, unreasonable or preposterous." For example, "What a ridiculous idea (or decision, job, costume, etc.)." To younger generations, *ridiculous* has come to mean something different: "awesome, extravagant or excessive." For example, "What a ridiculous car (or wedding, house, new bike, etc.)."

Curiously, both understandings of *ridiculous* fit Jesus as a Grace-Giver. His grace was at times preposterous and even absurd—totally undeserved. EVERY time it was extravagant and excessive. The seven lessons in this study reveal story after story of His **Ridiculous Grace**!

In our present-day American culture, grace has become an increasingly rare commodity. Instead of extending grace, people routinely extend harsh or insulting words in response to things or ideas they don't like. Instead of giving others the benefit of the doubt or seeking clarity, people jump to negative assumptions and conclusions that lead to judgment, anger, ugly words and ugly actions. Drive through your town or on a highway and you will see various levels of road rage; observe the way people talk to service agents at an airport or business and you will see disrespect; turn on the news and you will see regular examples of "grace-less" words and judgments.

Jesus modeled a very different way to live, and His life reveals something important about us: Our cultural sense of fair vs. unfair drives us. Deserved grace feels right and comfortable. Whether it's in words or action, ridiculous and undeserved grace shocks us. Jesus routinely extended **ridiculous grace**—extravagant, excessive, preposterous, unreasonable grace. We have much to learn from Him! We will be challenged by Him, and we will be blessed by Him, for we are recipients of His **Ridiculous Grace**!

Lessons 1–6 take place as Jesus began His travels from Capernaum to Jerusalem where He was to ultimately present Himself as the sacrifice for the sins of the world. As the lessons are not chronological, this map will help you place where each lesson happened (approximately). Lesson 7 takes place after Jesus rose from the dead.

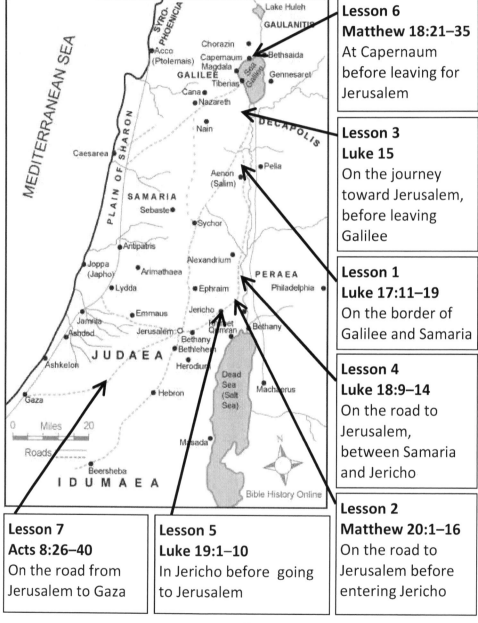

Lesson 6
Matthew 18:21–35
At Capernaum before leaving for Jerusalem

Lesson 3
Luke 15
On the journey toward Jerusalem, before leaving Galilee

Lesson 1
Luke 17:11–19
On the border of Galilee and Samaria

Lesson 4
Luke 18:9–14
On the road to Jerusalem, between Samaria and Jericho

Lesson 7
Acts 8:26–40
On the road from Jerusalem to Gaza

Lesson 5
Luke 19:1–10
In Jericho before going to Jerusalem

Lesson 2
Matthew 20:1–16
On the road to Jerusalem before entering Jericho

GRACE & GRATITUDE
Lesson 1
Luke 17:11–19

Experience the Story
Before you start answering this week's questions, slowly read **Luke 17:11–19**. Read it as you've never read it before. Imagine you're part of the story. What do you see? Hear? Feel? Do you see yourself in the story? Let the passage come alive for you, and then talk to God about what you noticed.

> ^{11} As Jesus continued on toward Jerusalem, he reached the border between Galilee and Samaria. ^{12} As he entered a village there, ten men with leprosy stood at a distance, ^{13} crying out, "Jesus, Master, have mercy on us!"
>
> ^{14} He looked at them and said, "Go show yourselves to the priests." And as they went, they were cleansed of their leprosy.
>
> ^{15} One of them, when he saw that he was healed, came back to Jesus, shouting, "Praise God!" ^{16} He fell to the ground at Jesus' feet, thanking him for what he had done. This man was a Samaritan.
>
> ^{17} Jesus asked, "Didn't I heal ten men? Where are the other nine? ^{18} Has no one returned to give glory to God except this foreigner?" ^{19} And Jesus said to the man, "Stand up and go. Your faith has healed you."

Background

Jesus had just left Galilee for the last time, which could not have been easy. After all, He had focused most of His ministry in Galilee and even established His home base in Capernaum, alongside the Sea of Galilee. He was headed toward Jerusalem, even though He knew full well that suffering awaited Him there. He took the most direct route, walking along the border between Galilee and Samaria.

With His ministry time running short, what He chose to teach and do was very significant. On one occasion during His travels He entered a village, and all of a sudden ten leprous men cried out for mercy.

The Big Idea

Some of the first words we teach children are "please" and "thank you." Sometimes parents even teach sign language for these words before their babies can talk. Why is this so important to us? Perhaps it's because these words set a tone of humility and respect. Or, perhaps parents want to teach an attitude of thankfulness from the youngest age. In this story we find that having and expressing gratitude was important to Jesus, too.

Dig In

1. Where was Jesus going and what route was He taking? (**17:11**)

2. From the following quote and Scriptures, explain why it was significant that Jesus chose to travel in a Samaritan area.
   a. After Assyria invaded Israel's Northern Kingdom and resettled it with its own people, the mixed race that developed became known as the Samaritans. "Pure-bred" Jews hated these "half-breeds" and the Samaritans in turn hated the Jews. So many tensions arose between the two peoples that Jewish travelers between Galilee and southern Judah often would walk around rather than through Samaritan territory, even though this would lengthen their trip considerably. Jesus held no such prejudices.[1]

---

[1] *Life Application Study Bible: New Living Translation*, Carol Stream, IL: Tyndale House, 2014. 1704

b. **Luke 9:52–56**

c. **Luke 10:25–37**

e. Summarize your thoughts about Jesus and Samaritans.

3. Who did Jesus encounter as He entered the village? (**Luke 17:12**)

   a. What are your thoughts on the following?
      They cried from a distance, because they were "unclean" and
      forbidden to touch healthy people. Furthermore, in that era it
      was assumed disease came from sin.[1] Consequently, everyone,
      including the lepers themselves, would have assumed they were
      sinners, unworthy of being close to Jesus.[2]

   b. Why do you think they were together?

   c. Describe the life of a leper in that day. Do a bit of research and
      share with your group.

---

[1] **John 9**
[2] Card, Michael. *Luke, The Gospel of Amazement*. IVP Books, 2011. 198

d. What did these lepers want? Imagine and then suggest what their tone of voice might have been. (**17:13**)

e. They called Jesus "Master." What does that tell you about them?

4. How did Jesus respond to the plea from the ten men? (**17:14**)

a. Was Jesus' method/instruction different in any way from His other healings? If so, how? (e.g., see **Luke 5:12–14**)

b. How did the men receive Jesus' instructions, and what happened to them? (**17:14**)

c. Consider your life and how you react when Jesus asks you to do something before you have evidence it will succeed (e.g., forgive someone, give generously by tithing, serve God in a new way, invite a friend to church or a small group, etc.). Discuss why this is difficult.

d. Why would Jesus want these lepers to go to a priest? How would that benefit them in their Jewish culture? Read **Leviticus 13:9** and **14:1–9** to inform your answer.

5. After their healing, what happened? (**Luke 17:15–16**)

a. What do the man's actions indicate to you about his emotions and his spiritual understanding?

b. What do you learn about his nationality from **verses 15–16**? Why is this fact important? What does the mention of it imply to you about the nine others?

6. Think about and comment on Jesus' reaction in **17:18–19**.[1]

a. Why do you think the other men didn't return to thank Jesus? What would you say about their faith?

---

[1] One of the major themes of Luke is the remarkable faith of Gentiles. Although many of the Jewish religious leaders rejected Jesus, a number of foreigners wholeheartedly placed their trust in Him. Barton, Bruce B., David Veerman, Linda Chaffee Taylor, and Grant R. Osborne. *Luke*. Wheaton, IL: Tyndale House, 1997. 399

b. Do you think the grateful man's faith was different? How?

c. Comment on the following: We could assume that Jesus felt hurt because nobody thanked Him. But I think He was disappointed for another reason. He tells the leper who came back, "Your faith has made you well." Ten were healed, but only one was made well, and that's far more important than being healed.[1]

d. How do you see people taking God's provision, whether tangible or intangible, for granted today? (i.e., food, finances, friends, freedom, faith, etc.)

  i. How do you take God's provision for granted or credit yourself with good outcomes?

  ii. Please list at least five mercies of God you've experienced this week. Thank the Lord as you write.

[1] Larson, Bruce. *The Communicator's Commentary*. Word Books, 1983. 242

7. What part does gratitude play in your faith and life today?

8. What do you observe about praise and gratitude in the following Psalms and prayers? Underline phrases or concepts that bring to mind things for which to be grateful.

a. **Psalm 8:3–9**

   ³ When I look at the night sky and see the work of your fingers—
   the moon and the stars you set in place—
   ⁴ what are mere mortals that you should think about them,
   human beings that you should care for them?
   ⁵ Yet you made them only a little lower than God
   and crowned them with glory and honor.
   ⁶ You gave them charge of everything you made,
   putting all things under their authority—
   ⁷ the flocks and the herds
   and all the wild animals,
   ⁸ the birds in the sky, the fish in the sea,
   and everything that swims the ocean currents.
   ⁹ O LORD, our Lord, your majestic name fills the earth!

b. **Psalm 103:1–5**

   ¹ Let all that I am praise the LORD;
   with my whole heart, I will praise his holy name.
   ² Let all that I am praise the LORD;
   may I never forget the good things he does for me.
   ³ He forgives all my sins
   and heals all my diseases.
   ⁴ He redeems me from death
   and crowns me with love and tender mercies.
   ⁵ He fills my life with good things.
   My youth is renewed like the eagle's!

c. **Psalm 145:3–10, 13–15**

> ³ *Great is the Lord! He is most worthy of praise!*
>   *No one can measure his greatness.*
> ⁴ *Let each generation tell its children of your mighty acts;*
>   *let them proclaim your power.*
> ⁵ *I will meditate on your majestic, glorious splendor*
>   *and your wonderful miracles.*
> ⁶ *Your awe-inspiring deeds will be on every tongue;*
>   *I will proclaim your greatness.*
> ⁷ *Everyone will share the story of your wonderful goodness;*
>   *they will sing with joy about your righteousness.*
> ⁸ *The Lord is merciful and compassionate,*
>   *slow to get angry and filled with unfailing love.*
> ⁹ *The Lord is good to everyone.*
>   *He showers compassion on all his creation.*
> ¹⁰ *All of your works will thank you, Lord,*
>   *and your faithful followers will praise you.*
> ¹³ *For your kingdom is an everlasting kingdom.*
>   *You rule throughout all generations.*
>   *The Lord always keeps his promises;*
>   *he is gracious in all he does.*
> ¹⁴ *The Lord helps the fallen*
>   *and lifts those bent beneath their loads.*
> ¹⁵ *The eyes of all look to you in hope;*
>   *you give them their food as they need it.*

d. What are your personal take-aways for your prayer life after pondering these Scriptures of praise, gratitude and thanksgiving?

Expand Your Understanding

1. After doing this lesson, what new or fresh thought (or thoughts) do you have about Jesus?

2. In light of this new or fresh thought (or thoughts), how would you describe Him to a friend?

3. How will this new or fresh thinking about Jesus affect your everyday life?

Prayer Requests

GRACE UNDESERVED
Lesson 2
Matthew 20:1–16

Experience the Story

Before you start answering this week's questions, slowly read **Matthew 20:1–16**. Read it as you've never read it before. Imagine you're part of the story. What do you see? Hear? Feel? Do you see yourself in the story? Let the passage come alive for you, and then talk to God about what you noticed.

¹ *"For the Kingdom of Heaven is like the landowner who went out early one morning to hire workers for his vineyard.* ² *He agreed to pay the normal daily wage and sent them out to work.*

³ *"At nine o'clock in the morning he was passing through the marketplace and saw some people standing around doing nothing.* ⁴ *So he hired them, telling them he would pay them whatever was right at the end of the day.* ⁵ *So they went to work in the vineyard. At noon and again at three o'clock he did the same thing.* ⁶ *"At five o'clock that afternoon he was in town again and saw some more people standing around. He asked them, 'Why haven't you been working today?'* ⁷ *"They replied, 'Because no one hired us.' "The landowner told them, 'Then go out and join the others in my vineyard.'*

⁸ *"That evening he told the foreman to call the workers in and pay them, beginning with the last workers first.* ⁹ *When those hired at five o'clock were paid, each received a full day's wage.* ¹⁰ *When those hired first came to get their pay, they assumed they would receive more. But they, too, were paid a day's wage.* ¹¹ *When they received their pay, they protested to the owner,* ¹² *'Those people worked only one hour, and yet you've paid them just as much as you paid us who worked all day in the scorching heat.'*

¹³ *"He answered one of them, 'Friend, I haven't been unfair! Didn't you agree to work all day for the usual wage?* ¹⁴ *Take your money and go. I wanted to pay this last worker the same as you.* ¹⁵ *Is it against the law for me to do what I want with my money? Should you be jealous because I am kind to others?'* ¹⁶ *"So those who are last now will be first then, and those who are first will be last."*

_____

_____

_____

_____

_____

_____

_____

_____

_____

Background

The Parable[1] of the Vineyard is set during the grape harvest in Palestine. Generally this harvest occurred in September and it was closely followed by the rainy season. As a result, landowners were eager to get as many workers as they could to complete the harvest in a timely manner. The rain would ruin the grapes. Any worker was welcome, even if he could only work an hour or two. Men who needed work waited in the marketplace, hoping to be hired. Some even stayed until late in the day, showing they were desperate for even a little bit of work before sunset to provide for their families.[2]

The Big Idea

Consider people you've known or even strangers you've seen who have been out of work and trying day after day to find a job. As their money runs out, they feel more and more desperate. Suppose such a person was hired for a half-time position at the place you've worked for years. Later you learn the new employee received the same pay and benefit package as you, a full-time employee. Such was the case in the Parable of the Vineyard.

_____

[1] "Merriam-Webster defines a parable as: a short fictitious story that illustrates a moral attitude or a religious principle.
[2] Barclay, William. *The Gospel of Matthew*. Volume 2. Louisville, KY: Westminster John Knox, 1975. 222–223

Dig In

1. Jesus launched this parable by saying, "For the Kingdom of Heaven is like..." This phrase is used 32 times in the Gospel of Matthew alone. What do you think the "Kingdom of Heaven" means?

   a. Read the following Scriptures and quote to help you further understand and describe it. Note your observations.

      i. **Matthew 5:3**
God blesses those who are poor and realize their need for him, for the Kingdom of Heaven is theirs.

      ii. **Matthew 5:10**
God blesses those who are persecuted for doing right, for the Kingdom of Heaven is theirs.

      iii. **Revelation 11:15**
Then the seventh angel blew his trumpet, and there were loud voices shouting in heaven: "The world has now become the Kingdom of our Lord and of his Christ, and he will reign forever and ever."

      iv. **Daniel 2:44**
During the reigns of those kings, the God of heaven will set up a kingdom that will never be destroyed or conquered. It will crush all these kingdoms into nothingness, and it will stand forever.

v. The Kingdom is not an abstract principle. It is God's rule actively invading the kingdom of Satan. The Old Testament looks forward to a single manifestation of God's kingdom when His glory will fill the earth and Satan will be completely defeated. That day will come. However, Jesus taught that the kingdom of God has also entered the present age to bring men and women the blessings of forgiveness (**Mark 2:5**), life (**John 3:3**), righteousness (**Matthew 5:20**; **Romans 14:16**) and deliverance from the power of darkness (**Colossians 1:13**) and the sway of evil.[1]

b. Why is it, or might it be, important to understand this term as you study the Parable of the Vineyard in **Matthew 20:1–16**?

2. At what times of day did the landowner hire workers?[2] (**Matthew 20:3–6**)

a. What was each of them paid?[3] (**20:8–10**)

b. Do you think the early morning workers were fairly paid? Why or why not?

---

[1] Elwell, Walter, General Editor. *Evangelical Dictionary of Theology*. Baker Book House, 1984. 608–610

[2] The third, sixth, ninth and eleventh hours are 9 a.m., noon, 3 p.m., and 5 p.m. (or an hour before sunset). Tasker, R. V. G. *The Gospel According to St. Matthew: An Introduction and Commentary*. Leicester: Inter-Varsity, 1961. Barker, Kenneth L., and John R. Kohlenberger. *Zondervan NIV Bible Commentary*. Grand Rapids, MI: Zondervan Pub. House, 1994. 91

[3] Payment had to be made at sunset every day, according to **Leviticus 19:13**.

c. How did those early morning workers respond?[1] (**20:11–12**)

d. Do you think they were unreasonable? Please explain your answer.

e. Why would Jesus be sure the last workers were paid first as He told the parable?

f. What do you think of the landowners response in **verses 13–15**?

g. What conclusion does Jesus draw in **verse 16**?

3. In this parable, who does the landowner represent?

a. Who do the hired workers represent?

b. What do you perceive is the overall message of this parable?

---

[1] The normal working day was 10 hours or so, not counting breaks. Barker, Kenneth L., and John R. Kohlenberger. *Zondervan NIV Bible Commentary*. Grand Rapids, MI: Zondervan Pub. House, 1994. 91

4. How do the following Scriptures underscore the message of the
   Parable of the Vineyard?
   a. **Luke 23:32–34, 39–43**
      *³² Two others, both criminals, were led out to be executed with him.
      ³³ When they came to a place called The Skull, they nailed him to
      the cross. And the criminals were also crucified—one on his right
      and one on his left. ³⁴ Jesus said, "Father, forgive them, for they
      don't know what they are doing." And the soldiers gambled for his
      clothes by throwing dice.*

      *³⁹ One of the criminals hanging beside him scoffed, "So you're the
      Messiah, are you? Prove it by saving yourself—and us, too, while
      you're at it!" ⁴⁰ But the other criminal protested, "Don't you fear
      God even when you have been sentenced to die? ⁴¹ We deserve
      to die for our crimes, but this man hasn't done anything wrong."
      ⁴² Then he said, "Jesus, remember me when you come into your
      Kingdom." ⁴³ And Jesus replied, "I assure you, today you will be with
      me in paradise.*

   b. **Acts 15:10–11**
      *¹⁰ So why are you now challenging God by burdening the Gentile
      believers with a yoke[1] that neither we nor our ancestors were able
      to bear? ¹¹ We believe that we are all saved the same way, by the
      undeserved grace of the Lord Jesus.*

   c. **Romans 11:5–6**
      *⁵... a few of the people of Israel have remained faithful because of
      God's grace—his undeserved kindness in choosing them. ⁶ And since
      it is through God's kindness, then it is not by their good works. For
      in that case, God's grace would not be what it really is—free and
      undeserved.*

---

[1] The yoke that some Jewish Christians were trying to put on Gentile Christians was the
requirement that they also be circumcised. (**Acts 15**)

d. **Ephesians 2:8**
   God saved you by his grace when you believed. And you can't take credit for this; it is a gift from God.

e. What do these Scriptures teach you about God's heart?

f. Summarize your conclusions about God's grace as it relates to the Parable of the Vineyard.

5. "In the Kingdom of God, the driving force is not merit and ability (as it is in the world) but grace."[1] List examples of how this thinking differs from the world around you and from your life experience.

a. Summarize your conclusions about God's saving grace in YOUR life. What was going on in your life when He redeemed you?

---

[1] Barker, Kenneth L., and John R. Kohlenberger. *Zondervan NIV Bible Commentary*. Grand Rapids, MI: Zondervan Pub. House, 1994. 91

b. List several other ways you've experienced God's undeserved grace in the last year. Be as specific as you can.

6. What can/does make you reluctant to share the grace of God?

   a. Why?

   b. How has this study affected your perspective?

   c. *When he saw the crowds, Jesus had compassion on them because they were confused and helpless, like sheep without a shepherd. He said to his disciples, "The harvest is great, but the workers are few. So pray to the Lord who is in charge of the harvest; ask him to send more workers into his fields."* (**Matthew 9:36–38**)

      How do Jesus' words inspire you?

   d. Take five minutes right now and ask God to change your heart and make it like His.

e. Who is God bringing to mind; someone who needs to hear the glorious news of His saving grace? As a group and using first names only, pray for the individuals you've identified. God is all-knowing and will know who they are.

Expand Your Understanding

1. After doing this lesson, what new or fresh thought (or thoughts) do you have about Jesus?

2. In light of this new or fresh thought (or thoughts), how would you describe Him to a friend?

3. How will this new or fresh thinking about Jesus affect your everyday life?

Prayer Requests

GRACE FOUND
Lesson 3
Luke 15

Experience the Story

Before you start answering this week's questions, slowly read **Luke 15**. Read it as you've never read it before. Imagine you're part of the story. What do you see? Hear? Feel? Do you see yourself in the story? Let the passage come alive for you, and then talk to God about what you noticed.

¹ *Tax collectors and other notorious sinners often came to listen to Jesus teach.* ² *This made the Pharisees and teachers of religious law complain that he was associating with such sinful people—even eating with them!*

³ *So Jesus told them this story:* ⁴ *"If a man has a hundred sheep and one of them gets lost, what will he do? Won't he leave the ninety-nine others in the wilderness and go to search for the one that is lost until he finds it?* ⁵ *And when he has found it, he will joyfully carry it home on his shoulders.* ⁶ *When he arrives, he will call together his friends and neighbors, saying, 'Rejoice with me because I have found my lost sheep.'* ⁷ *In the same way, there is more joy in heaven over one lost sinner who repents and returns to God than over ninety-nine others who are righteous and haven't strayed away!*

⁸ *"Or suppose a woman has ten silver coins and loses one. Won't she light a lamp and sweep the entire house and search carefully until she finds it?* ⁹ *And when she finds it, she will call in her friends and neighbors and say, 'Rejoice with me because I have found my lost coin.'* ¹⁰ *In the same way, there is joy in the presence of God's angels when even one sinner repents."*

¹¹ *To illustrate the point further, Jesus told them this story: "A man had two sons.* ¹² *The younger son told his father, 'I want my share of your estate now before you die.' So his father agreed to divide his wealth between his sons.*

¹³ *"A few days later this younger son packed all his belongings and moved to a distant land, and there he wasted all his money in wild living.* ¹⁴ *About the time his money ran out, a great famine swept over the land, and he began to starve.* ¹⁵ *He persuaded a local farmer to hire him, and the man sent him into his fields to feed the pigs.* ¹⁶ *The young man became so hungry that even the pods he was feeding the pigs looked good to him. But no one gave him anything.*

_17_ "When he finally came to his senses, he said to himself, 'At home even the hired servants have food enough to spare, and here I am dying of hunger! _18_ I will go home to my father and say, "Father, I have sinned against both heaven and you, _19_ and I am no longer worthy of being called your son. Please take me on as a hired servant."'_

_20_ "So he returned home to his father. And while he was still a long way off, his father saw him coming. Filled with love and compassion, he ran to his son, embraced him, and kissed him. _21_ His son said to him, 'Father, I have sinned against both heaven and you, and I am no longer worthy of being called your son.'_

_22_ "But his father said to the servants, 'Quick! Bring the finest robe in the house and put it on him. Get a ring for his finger and sandals for his feet. _23_ And kill the calf we have been fattening. We must celebrate with a feast, _24_ for this son of mine was dead and has now returned to life. He was lost, but now he is found.' So the party began._

_25_ "Meanwhile, the older son was in the fields working. When he returned home, he heard music and dancing in the house, _26_ and he asked one of the servants what was going on. _27_ 'Your brother is back,' he was told, 'and your father has killed the fattened calf. We are celebrating because of his safe return.'_

_28_ "The older brother was angry and wouldn't go in. His father came out and begged him, _29_ but he replied, 'All these years I've slaved for you and never once refused to do a single thing you told me to. And in all that time you never gave me even one young goat for a feast with my friends. _30_ Yet when this son of yours comes back after squandering your money on prostitutes, you celebrate by killing the fattened calf!'_

_31_ "His father said to him, 'Look, dear son, you have always stayed by me, and everything I have is yours. _32_ We had to celebrate this happy day. For your brother was dead and has come back to life! He was lost, but now he is found!'"_

Background

Jesus and His disciples were slowly making their way to Jerusalem. They stopped in at towns and villages along the way, performing miracles and teaching truth. Sometimes Jesus taught in synagogues, and other times crowds materialized around Him. Either way, whether Jesus sought people out or people sought Him out, He engaged deeply and shared God's grace with them.

Some of those listening to Jesus, the Pharisees, did not like what they heard Him preach and oftentimes tried to trick, trap or discredit Him. One of their biggest complaints was that Jesus associated with social outcasts and notorious sinners[1]—people they despised and considered beyond hope. In this lesson we find Jesus yet again confronting the Pharisees about their critical spirit toward people, which was in stark contrast to the grace that God offers EVERYONE.

The Big Idea

Have you ever lost something that makes you drop everything in your life until you find it? Think of what would happen in your heart, mind and body if all of a sudden you realized your child, or the child of a friend or relative you are in charge of, went missing. You would be frantic, your heart would race, you would start sweating, and you would immediately stop everything until they were found! Your heart's desire would be to have them back in your arms, to tell them how much you love them, and to reassure them they are safe!

God feels this way about those who are far from Him. He is desperate to be in relationship with them, in order to lavish grace on them. He longs to take them in His arms and reassure them they are safe and loved. In Luke 15, Jesus used three parables[2] about things that were lost and then found to demonstrate His heart. Each one shows His love for ALL people. He actively searches for them and longs to restore them to relationship and give them His abundant grace.

---

[1] **Luke 5:30; 7:39**
[2] Merriam-Webster defines a parable as: a short fictitious story that illustrates a moral attitude or a religious principle.

Dig In

1. The first of these three parables is found in **Luke 15:3–7**. Read through it a few times. What did the shepherd in Jesus' story do when he realized one of his many sheep was missing?[1]

   What did the shepherd do when he found it? Who shared in his joy? (**15:5–6**)

2. Based on **verse 7**, what is the spiritual reality Jesus announced?

   a. The shepherd left the 99 sheep to rescue the one that was lost. Jesus left heaven to rescue all of humanity. What does/would it look like for you leave something behind to pursue those in need of God's grace?

   b. How do you rejoice when someone is found and experiences the amazing grace of Christ? Or do you? (**15:6**)

      i. What could real rejoicing look like? Let images from the parable help give you creative ideas.

---

[1] Sheep were of significant commercial value. Wilkins, Michael J. *Matthew: From Biblical Text to Contemporary Life*. Grand Rapids, MI: Zondervan, 2004.

    ii. Perhaps we would have more joy in our churches if we shared Jesus' love and concern for the lost, diligently seeking them, rejoicing when they come to the Savior.[1] Now imagine what this could look like in your life and in the life of your church. Process with your group some practical ways to rejoice.

  c. Our God actively searches for the lost. Underline what you learn about God's character in the following Scriptures. Share with your group.

    i. **Isaiah 40:10–11**

> [10] *Yes, the Sovereign LORD is coming in power.*
> *He will rule with a powerful arm.*
> *See, he brings his reward with him as he comes.*
> [11] *He will feed his flock like a shepherd.*
> *He will carry the lambs in his arms,*
> *holding them close to his heart.*
> *He will gently lead the mother sheep with their young.*

    ii. **John 10:14–16**

> [14] *"I am the good shepherd; I know my own sheep, and they know me,* [15] *just as my Father knows me and I know the Father. So I sacrifice my life for the sheep.* [16] *I have other sheep, too, that are not in this sheepfold. I must bring them also. They will listen to my voice, and there will be one flock with one shepherd."*

3. The second parable that Jesus told the Pharisees was about a woman who had ten coins and lost one. Read **Luke 15:8–10**. What did she do when she realized one of her coins was lost?

---

[1] *Life Application Study Bible: New Living Translation*, Carol Stream, IL: Tyndale House, 2014. 1719

a. She had nine out of ten coins. Normally 90% would be satisfactory, yet she was frantic for the one she lost. What does that tell you about God's heart?

b. Who did she recruit to join her in her celebration when she found the lost coin?

4. Who did Jesus claim is celebrating when a sinner repents? **(15:10)**

a. Why would angels be highlighted here?

b. Imagine what angels rejoicing would look like. Have fun with this and note your ideas.[1]

5. The final parable Jesus told the Pharisees was the Parable of the Lost Son (**Luke 15:11–32**). Many know this as the Parable of the Prodigal Son. While this may be a familiar story, try to read it as if for the first time. As you do, note the thoughts and emotions you experience as you read.

---

[1] If you like cross references, see **Revelation 7:11–12**

a. Describe the actions and attitudes of the following:
    i. The younger son

    ii. The older son

    iii. The father

    iv. Which one do you most relate to?

b. Most of us find admitting wrongs and repenting to be very hard. How does God's character revealed in these three parables encourage you toward repentance?[1]

6. God longs for us to repent and come to Him. He is a patient Father, willing to wait. What do you learn about Him in the following Scriptures?
    a. **Isaiah 30:18**
       So the LORD must wait for you to come to him
         so he can show you his love and compassion.
       For the LORD is a faithful God.
         Blessed are those who wait for his help.

    b. **2 Peter 3:9**
       The Lord isn't really being slow about his promise, as some people think. No, he is being patient for your sake. He does not want anyone to be destroyed, but wants everyone to repent.

---

[1] Repenting is to show regret and to turn away from the sin.

7. How do you tend to respond to those who need grace and those who have responded to grace? Are you more like the father or the older brother?

a. Interact with this quote: "Once Lincoln was asked how he was going to treat the rebellious southerners when they had finally been defeated and had returned to the Union of the United States. The questioner expected that Lincoln would take a dire vengeance, but he answered, 'I will treat them as if they had never been away.' It is the wonder of the love of God that he treats us like that."[1]

b. Who is it in your life or sphere of influence that needs God's grace? How can you pursue them with the grace God has to offer?

---

[1] Barclay, William. *The Gospel of Luke*. Louisville, KY: Westminster John Knox, 2001. 205

Expand Your Understanding

1. After doing this lesson, what new or fresh thought (or thoughts) do you have about Jesus?

2. In light of this new or fresh thought (or thoughts), how would you describe Him to a friend?

3. How will this new or fresh thinking about Jesus affect your everyday life?

Prayer Requests

GRACE & HUMILITY
Lesson 4
Luke 18:9–14

Experience the Story

Before you start answering this week's questions, slowly read **Luke 18:9–14**. Read it as you've never read it before. Imagine you're part of the story. What do you see? Hear? Feel? Do you see yourself in the story? Let the passage come alive for you, and then talk to God about what you noticed.

⁹ Then Jesus told this story to some who had great confidence in their own righteousness and scorned everyone else: ¹⁰ "Two men went to the Temple to pray. One was a Pharisee, and the other was a despised tax collector. ¹¹ The Pharisee stood by himself and prayed this prayer: 'I thank you, God, that I am not like other people—cheaters, sinners, adulterers. I'm certainly not like that tax collector! ¹² I fast twice a week, and I give you a tenth of my income.'

¹³ "But the tax collector stood at a distance and dared not even lift his eyes to heaven as he prayed. Instead, he beat his chest in sorrow, saying, 'O God, be merciful to me, for I am a sinner.' ¹⁴ I tell you, this sinner, not the Pharisee, returned home justified before God. For those who exalt themselves will be humbled, and those who humble themselves will be exalted."

_____

_____

_____

_____

_____

_____

_____

_____

_____

Background

Just like our previous lessons, Jesus and His disciples were traveling between Samaria and Galilee toward Jericho and ultimately to Jerusalem. On the way, Jesus stopped frequently to teach the crowds and perform miracles. This particular passage is one of the many parables Jesus told during this journey. Conceptually, Jesus had been teaching the people that they should always pray and not lose hope. In this reading, Jesus continued His teaching on prayer, explaining HOW to approach God.

Setting the Scene

Is pride a good thing or a bad thing? On one hand, we've all heard parents tell their kids to "take pride" in their schoolwork or chores. This seems to imply that, sometimes, how well one does a task is a reflection of that person's character. On the other hand, we have all heard the old adage, "pride comes before a fall."[1] This seems to suggest that having too much pride can lead to a serious life malfunction! How are we to know how much is too much? Too little? Maybe a better question is: What does God have to say about pride? In this parable, we'll discover what Jesus taught concerning pride and humility.

Dig In

1. According to **verse 9**, who was the intended audience of this parable?

    a. What does this opening line say about the audience to whom Jesus was speaking?

    b. The text says that these people had "great confidence in their own righteousness and scorned everyone else." Why might trusting in our own righteousness cause us to look down on others?

---

[1] Fun Fact! This old saying actually originates from the Old Testament book of Proverbs: *Pride goes before destruction, and haughtiness before a fall.* (**Proverbs 16:18**)

34

c. Where do you see self-righteousness or scorning[1] others in our culture today?

2. Who are the two characters in this story? (**18:10**)

a. Read **Luke 5:17–31** and underline anything that helps you understand more about Pharisees and Tax Collectors.

[17] One day while Jesus was teaching, some Pharisees and teachers of religious law were sitting nearby. (It seemed that these men showed up from every village in all Galilee and Judea, as well as from Jerusalem.) And the Lord's healing power was strongly with Jesus. [18] Some men came carrying a paralyzed man on a sleeping mat. They tried to take him inside to Jesus, [19] but they couldn't reach him because of the crowd. So they went up to the roof and took off some tiles. Then they lowered the sick man on his mat down into the crowd, right in front of Jesus. [20] Seeing their faith, Jesus said to the man, "Young man, your sins are forgiven." [21] But the Pharisees and teachers of religious law said to themselves, "Who does he think he is? That's blasphemy! Only God can forgive sins!" [22] Jesus knew what they were thinking, so he asked them, "Why do you question this in your hearts? [23] Is it easier to say 'Your sins are forgiven,' or 'Stand up and walk'? [24] So I will prove to you that the Son of Man has the authority on earth to forgive sins." Then Jesus turned to the paralyzed man and said, "Stand up, pick up your mat, and go home!" [25] And immediately, as everyone watched, the man jumped up, picked up his mat, and went home praising God. [26] Everyone was gripped with great wonder and awe, and they praised God, exclaiming, "We have seen amazing things today!" [27] Later, as Jesus left the town, he saw a tax collector named Levi sitting at his tax collector's booth. "Follow me and be my disciple," Jesus said to him. [28] So Levi got up, left everything, and followed him. [29] Later, Levi held a banquet in his home with Jesus as the guest of honor. Many of Levi's fellow tax collectors and other guests also ate with them. [30] But the Pharisees and their teachers of religious law complained bitterly to Jesus' disciples, "Why do you eat and drink with such scum?" [31] Jesus answered

---

[1] Merriam-Webster defines scorn as: having feelings that someone or something is not worthy of any respect or approval.

them, *"Healthy people don't need a doctor—sick people do.* ³² *I have come to call not those who think they are righteous, but those who know they are sinners and need to repent."*

    b. Why do you think Jesus decided to use these two characters for this parable in **Luke 18:9–14**?

3. As the Pharisee prayed, what catches your eye in his demeanor and prayer (**11–12**)? Write three things you observed.

    a. Read the following passages from the Old Testament with the Pharisee's prayer in mind. Note your thoughts.

      i. **Ezra 8:21**

      "... I (Ezra) gave orders for all of us to fast and humble ourselves before our God. We prayed that he would give us a safe journey and protect us..."[1]

      ii. **Malachi 3:8–10**

      ⁸ *(God says) "Should people cheat God? Yet you have cheated me!" (Israel responds) "What do you mean? When did we ever cheat you?" (God responds)* ⁹ *"You have cheated me of the tithes and offerings due to me.* ¹⁰ *You are under a curse, for your whole nation has been cheating me. Bring all the tithes into the storehouse so there will be enough food in my Temple.*

---

[1] The journey being addressed here is the trip from their exile in Babylon back to the Promised Land.

If you do...I will open the windows of heaven for you. I will pour out my blessing so great you won't have room enough to take it in!"

b. In light of these Old Testament passages, would you consider the Pharisee's actions in this story to be righteous or unrighteous? Was he following the rules?[1]

4. Read the tax collector's prayer in **Luke 18:13**. What catches your eye in his demeanor and words?

a. Compare and contrast the tax collector's prayer and the Pharisee's **(18:11–12)**. Write three things you observed.

b. The Pharisee followed the laws of God perfectly.[2] So why did Jesus pronounce the tax collector as "justified before God" **(18:14)** if he didn't follow "the rules"?

---

[1] "The Jewish law prescribed only one absolutely obligatory fast—on the Day of Atonement (see **Leviticus 16**). But those who wished to gain special merit fasted also on Monday and Thursday." Barclay, William. *The Gospel of Luke*. Louisville, KY: Westminster John Knox, 2001. 223-224

[2] According to the excessive pharisaical religious standards, the Pharisee actually fulfilled the Law and then some.

c. What did the tax collector have that the Pharisee didn't? (**18:14**)

d. Note two or three ways a humble attitude can overcome self-righteousness and pride.

5. What does God want from us? It turns out, God had been dealing with prideful people long before the Pharisees. The prophet Isaiah recorded God's harsh response to those who trusted in their pious and prideful worship instead of coming to Him with a humble heart. Read the following excerpt from **Isaiah 58** and ponder the role of humility in your life.

> ³ 'We have fasted before you!' they say.
>   'Why aren't you impressed?
> We have been very hard on ourselves,
>   and you don't even notice it!'
> "I will tell you why!" I [God] respond.
>   "It's because you are fasting to please yourselves.
> Even while you fast,
>   you keep oppressing your workers.
> ⁴ What good is fasting
>   when you keep on fighting and quarreling?
> This kind of fasting
>   will never get you anywhere with me.
> ⁵ You humble yourselves
>   by going through the motions of penance,
> bowing your heads
>   like reeds bending in the wind.
> You dress in burlap
>   and cover yourselves with ashes.
> Is this what you call fasting?
>   Do you really think this will please the LORD?

a. Based on this passage, why does God desire humility?

b. How does **Isaiah 58** speak specifically to your attitudes, actions and worship?

6. Re-read **Luke 18:14**. Why is it hard to receive God's gracious gift of justification if we don't approach Him with a humble heart?

a. Read the following excerpt about humbly receiving grace from the Apostle Paul's letter to his Christian friends living in Rome. (**Romans 3:21–24; 4:27–28**)

> *21 "But now God has shown us a way to be made right with him without keeping the requirements of the law, as was promised in the writings of Moses, and the prophets long ago. 22 We are made right with God by placing our faith in Jesus Christ. And this is true for everyone who believes, no matter who we are. 23 For everyone has sinned; we all fall short of God's glorious standard. 24 Yet God, in his grace, freely makes us right in his sight. He did this through Christ Jesus when he freed us from the penalty for our sins. 27 Can we boast, then, that we have done anything to be accepted by God? No, because our acquittal is not based on obeying the law. It is based on faith. 28 So we are made right with God through faith and not by obeying the law 29 After all, is God the God of the Jews only? Isn't he also the God of the Gentiles? Of course he is. 30 There is only one God, and he makes people right with himself only by faith, whether they are Jews or Gentiles. 31 Well then, if we emphasize faith, does this mean that we can forget about the law? Of course not! In fact, only when we have faith do we truly fulfill the law.*

b. Note your thoughts:

7. The beautiful truth about the story of the Pharisee and tax collector is that God can save (and LOVES!) even the worst person (**Luke 18**). His grace extends to the depths of our sinful behaviors, thoughts, words and motives and covers them all. However, the only thing He requires of us in return is a humble heart of faith and recognition of our sins.

   a. In your own life, what are some areas in which you hold on to pride like the Pharisee?

   b. How could a humble heart enable us to love others better?

   c. What would this look like in your life?

   d. Will you stop here and ask God to help you?

8. Along with learning from the Scriptures, we also have the great privilege of learning from the faithful men and women of the Church throughout history. John Wesley, an 18th century pastor and theologian, recognized the importance of a humble heart in response to God's great love for His people. Wesley wrote the following prayer with this in mind. Underline phrases that inspire, teach or challenge you.

> "We humble ourselves, O Lord of heaven and earth, before your glorious Majesty. We acknowledge your eternal power, wisdom, goodness, and truth; and desire to render you most unfeigned[1] thanks, for all the benefits which you pour upon us; but above all, for your inestimable love, in the redemption of the world by our Lord Jesus Christ. We implore your tender mercies in the forgiveness of all our sins, whereby we have offended either in thought, word, or deed. We desire to be truly sorry for all our misdoings, and utterly to renounce whatsoever is contrary to your will. We desire to devote our whole self, body, soul, and spirit, to you. And as you inspire us with these desires, so accompany them always with your grace, so that we may every day, with our whole hearts, give ourselves up to your service. We desire to be so holy and undefiled as our blessed Master was. And we trust you will fulfill all the gracious promises, which he has made to us. Let them be dearer to us than thousands of gold and silver; let them be the comfort and joy of our hearts. We ask nothing, but that it may be unto your servants according to his Word."

a. Share with each other what you underlined and why.

b. How does Wesley's humility instruct or inspire you?

c. If comfortable, pray this prayer as a group.

---

[1] Dictionary.com defines "unfeigned" as "genuine or sincere."

Expand Your Understanding

1. After doing this lesson, what new or fresh thought (or thoughts) do you have about Jesus?

2. In light of this new or fresh thought (or thoughts), how would you describe Him to a friend?

3. How will this new or fresh thinking about Jesus affect your everyday life?

Prayer Requests

TRANSFORMED BY GRACE
Lesson 5
Luke 19:1–10

Experience the Story

Before you start answering this week's questions, slowly read **Luke 19:1–10**. Read it as you've never read it before. Imagine you're part of the story. What do you see? Hear? Feel? Do you see yourself in the story? Let the passage come alive for you, and then talk to God about what you noticed.

> *¹ Jesus entered Jericho and made his way through the town. ² There was a man there named Zacchaeus. He was the chief tax collector in the region, and he had become very rich. ³ He tried to get a look at Jesus, but he was too short to see over the crowd. ⁴ So he ran ahead and climbed a sycamore-fig tree beside the road, for Jesus was going to pass that way.*
>
> *⁵ When Jesus came by, he looked up at Zacchaeus and called him by name. "Zacchaeus!" he said. "Quick, come down! I must be a guest in your home today."*
>
> *⁶ Zacchaeus quickly climbed down and took Jesus to his house in great excitement and joy. ⁷ But the people were displeased. "He has gone to be the guest of a notorious sinner," they grumbled.*
>
> *⁸ Meanwhile, Zacchaeus stood before the Lord and said, "I will give half my wealth to the poor, Lord, and if I have cheated people on their taxes, I will give them back four times as much!"*
>
> *⁹ Jesus responded, "Salvation has come to this home today, for this man has shown himself to be a true son of Abraham. ¹⁰ For the Son of Man came to seek and save those who are lost."*

_____

_____

_____

_____

_____

_____

_____

Background

In this story Jesus had finally entered Jericho on His way to Jerusalem. Word about Him had spread to the villages and cities, and they knew He was a great teacher, healing people and driving out demons. Jericho was a wealthy and important town; it had a great palm forest and world-famous balsam groves. The Romans carried its dates and balsam to worldwide trade and fame. Therefore, it was one of the greatest taxation centers in Palestine.[1] All of this had led to Zacchaeus' great wealth.

The Big Idea

Have you ever had a moment that changed the trajectory of your life? For example, something like a wedding, a death, or a birth. Maybe it was an interaction with a teacher that caused you to pursue a different degree and now you have a career you love. Maybe a comment from a friend caused you to realize you were heading down a dangerous road. Maybe it was the realization that you are desperately loved by the God of the universe and you decided to make him Lord of your life. Many of us can pinpoint a few moments in our lives that were life-changing. Zacchaeus had one of those moments. It was when he met Jesus, God incarnate. Zacchaeus' life was changed from that moment on.

Dig In

1. In the church community, the story of Zacchaeus is well-known to many. The story is even a children's song. However, we often miss that this is an account of how Jesus interacted with someone who was wildly unpopular in his time. Notice how Jesus saw Zacchaeus differently.

   a. What was Zacchaeus' job? (**19:2**)

   b. How had his job benefitted him?

---

[1] Barclay, William. *The Gospel of Luke*. Louisville, KY: Westminster John Knox, 2001. 234

c. What is your impression of how Zacchaeus was viewed by society?[1] (See **verses 6–7** and the footnote below)

  i. What might be a modern-day example of how society viewed Zacchaeus?

  ii. How does this affect the way you read this story?

2. Put yourself in Zacchaeus' shoes. You are in the back of a crowd trying desperately to see Jesus. What was Zacchaeus' solution to his problem? **(19:4)**

  a. What would your reaction be if you saw a well-known person running ahead of a crowd and climbing a tree in order to see someone?

  b. Has your desire to get to know Jesus ever caused you to do things that may be perceived as surprising or "out-of-the-box"? If yes, what are those things? If no, why not?

---

[1] To finance their great world empire, the Romans levied heavy taxes on all nations under their control. The Jews opposed these taxes because they supported a secular government and its pagan gods, but they were still forced to pay. Tax collectors were among the most unpopular people in Israel. Jews by birth, they chose to work for Rome and were considered traitors. Besides, it was common knowledge that tax collectors were making themselves rich by gouging their fellow Jews. *Life Application Study Bible: New Living Translation*, Carol Stream, IL: Tyndale House, 2014. 1727

3. Read **Luke 19:5–7**. What do you notice about Jesus?

    a. What do you notice about Zacchaeus?[1]

    b. What do you notice about the crowds?

        i. Review your response to question 1. c. i. (page 46) and answer the following. Do you identify with how the crowd was feeling? If so, how? Discuss with your group.

        ii. How do the crowds remind you of the older brother in the lost son story in lesson three?

        iii. When have you responded with judgment when you saw something good happen to someone you didn't like?

        iv. Respond to this quote: "The people who were most unlike Jesus liked Jesus and He liked them back."[2] **(19:5)**

---

[1] This word "great excitement and joy" is literally "rejoicing." Luke used this verb (and the noun *chara*) nine times to denote an attitude of joy accompanying faith and salvation. Walvoord, John F., and Roy B. Zuck. *The Bible Knowledge Commentary: An Exposition of the Scriptures.* CO Springs, CO: Victor, an Imprint of Cook Communications Ministries, 2004. 252

[2] Steve Fowler, Lead Pastor of Salem Alliance Church. April 30, 2017.

4. How do you think it would have impacted Zacchaeus emotionally (heart and head) to be called by name?

   a. Read the following verses and respond to the questions below.
      i. **Psalm 139:13–14, 17**
        ¹³ You made all the delicate, inner parts of my body and knit me together in my mother's womb. ¹⁴ Thank you for making me so wonderfully complex! Your workmanship is marvelous—how well I know it. ¹⁷ How precious are your thoughts about me, O God. They cannot be numbered.

      ii. **Matthew 10:29–31**
        ²⁹ What is the price of two sparrows—one copper coin? But not a single sparrow can fall to the ground without your Father knowing it. ³⁰ And the very hairs on your head are all numbered. ³¹ So don't be afraid; you are more valuable to God than a whole flock of sparrows.

     iii. **John 10:3**
        The gatekeeper opens the gate for him, and the sheep recognize his voice and come to him. He calls his own sheep by name and leads them out.

   b. What do these verses say about God's interest in your life?

   c. How does His interest impact your emotions (heart and head)?

5. What was Zacchaeus' response to Jesus in **Luke 19:8**?

    a. What do you think it was about Jesus that caused Zacchaeus' response?

    b. Zacchaeus' thinking was radically changed through an encounter with Jesus, and as a result, it changed the way he lived. Describe ways this has happened in your life. Share with your group.

6. Notice the language Jesus used in **verse 9**. What grace was given to Zacchaeus?

"This tax collector was perceived as a traitor by his people, so they would not have considered him a son of Abraham."[1]
In light of this quote, how would the Jews have responded to the salvation offered to Zacchaeus?[2]

7. Look at **Luke 19:10**, how would you rewrite that sentence?

---

[1] Barton, Bruce B., David Veerman, Linda Chaffee Taylor, and Grant R. Osborne. *Luke.* Wheaton, IL: Tyndale House, 1997. 432
[2] Being a true Son of Abraham means being a part of the family of God. Zacchaeus would have been excluded from this because of how he lived his life.

a. Is there anyone you would just as soon not receive salvation? Who?

b. Read and respond to **2 Peter 3:9**

   The Lord isn't really being slow about his promise as some people think. No, he is being patient for your sake. He does not want anyone to be destroyed, but wants everyone to repent.

c. What would change in your everyday life if you truly believed that no one was beyond Jesus' loving reach, including yourself? (i.e., would you pray for someone more, would you be willing to interact with others, would you befriend a neighbor or coworker, etc.)

Expand Your Understanding

1. After doing this lesson, what new or fresh thought (or thoughts) do you have about Jesus?

2. In light of this new or fresh thought (or thoughts), how would you describe Him to a friend?

3. How will this new or fresh thinking about Jesus affect your everyday life?

Prayer Requests

GRACE TO FORGIVE
Lesson 6
Matthew 18:21–35

Experience the Story
Before you start answering this week's questions, slowly read **Matthew 18:21–35**. Read it as you've never read it before. Imagine you're part of the story. What do you see? Hear? Feel? Do you see yourself in the story? Let the passage come alive for you, and then talk to God about what you noticed.

> ²¹ *Then Peter came to him and asked, "Lord, how often should I forgive someone who sins against me? Seven times?" ²² "No, not seven times," Jesus replied, "but seventy times seven!*
> ²³ *"Therefore, the Kingdom of Heaven can be compared to a king who decided to bring his accounts up to date with servants who had borrowed money from him. ²⁴ In the process, one of his debtors was brought in who owed him millions of dollars. ²⁵ He couldn't pay, so his master ordered that he be sold—along with his wife, his children, and everything he owned—to pay the debt.*
> ²⁶ *"But the man fell down before his master and begged him, 'Please, be patient with me, and I will pay it all.' ²⁷ Then his master was filled with pity for him, and he released him and forgave his debt.*
> ²⁸ *"But when the man left the king, he went to a fellow servant who owed him a few thousand dollars. He grabbed him by the throat and demanded instant payment.*
> ²⁹ *"His fellow servant fell down before him and begged for a little more time. 'Be patient with me, and I will pay it,' he pleaded. ³⁰ But his creditor wouldn't wait. He had the man arrested and put in prison until the debt could be paid in full.*
> ³¹ *"When some of the other servants saw this, they were very upset. They went to the king and told him everything that had happened. ³² Then the king called in the man he had forgiven and said, 'You evil servant! I forgave you that tremendous debt because you pleaded with me. ³³ Shouldn't you have mercy on your fellow servant, just as I had mercy on you?' ³⁴ Then the angry king sent the man to prison to be tortured until he had paid his entire debt.*
> ³⁵ *"That's what my heavenly Father will do to you if you refuse to forgive your brothers and sisters from your heart."*

_____

_____

_____

_____

_____

_____

_____

_____

_____

Background

Jesus and His disciples were in Capernaum, Jesus' ministry headquarters. These were His final moments at "home." Therefore, His teaching was among His last before they packed up and started their long trek toward Jerusalem and His ultimate sacrifice. Forgiveness and reconciliation were high on His priority list. Jesus wanted to make sure they got this right.

Set the Scene

The average American family that has credit card debt owes about $16,000. That's in addition to the $27,000 for auto loans and $48,000 for student loans.[1] According to *USA Today* it could take 14 or more years to pay off just the credit cards (and that's if no more debt is added to it).[2] You may be in debt yourself or know someone who is struggling to stay afloat. Now imagine if the companies, schools, etc. that are owed money decided to wipe the debt clean. As of today, nothing would be owed. Just think about the freedom, relief and joy that would bring. In the Parable of the Unforgiving Debtor, Jesus compared financial debt to sin debt. All those who accept the gift of His sacrifice on the cross would have their sin debt wiped completely clean. Wow! Freedom, relief, joy!

_____

[1] http://www.slate.com/articles/business/the_united_states_of_debt/2016
[2] www.usatoday.com/story/money/personalfinance/2016

Dig In

1. How would you describe forgiveness? Use a dictionary to research the word "forgive."

    a. According to rabbinic teaching, based on Old Testament passages,[1] people were only required to forgive someone who wronged them three times.[2] What does that tell you about Peter's question to Jesus about how many times they should forgive? (**Matthew 18:21**)

    b. What was Jesus' surprising response to Peter in **verse 22**? What did it imply?

    c. How does this principle impact you?[3] Does it irritate you? Overwhelm you? Relieve you?

    d. Thoughtfully consider and discuss with your group why forgiveness can be so hard.

---

[1] **Amos 1:3, 6, 9, 11, 13; 2:1, 4, 6; Job 33:29–30**

[2] *Life Application Study Bible: New Living Translation*, Carol Stream, IL: Tyndale House, 2014. 1581

[3] Some versions of the Scriptures say seventy-seven times and others say seventy times seven.

2. Jesus illustrated His point by telling a story in **Matthew 18:23–27**. What did He declare in **verse 23**?[1]

    a. How would you describe the actions and attitude of the servant? **(24–26)**

    b. How did the king respond? **(27)**

3. The story takes an interesting turn in **verses 28–30**. What did the forgiven servant do?

4. How did the forgiven man's fellow servants react to his demands on his debtor (who only owed him three months wages)?

    a. What are your thoughts about their actions?

    b. What did the king declare to the servant he had forgiven? **(32–33)**

---

[1] The Kingdom is not an abstract principle. It is God's rule actively invading the kingdom of Satan. The Old Testament looks forward to a single manifestation of God's kingdom when His glory will fill the earth and Satan will be completely defeated. That day will come. However, Jesus taught that the kingdom of God has also entered the present age to bring men and women the blessings of forgiveness (**Mark 2:5**), life (**John 3:3**), righteousness (**Matthew 5:20; Romans 14:16**), deliverance from the power of darkness (**Colossians 1:13**) and from the sway of evil.

c. Where did the king send the servant?[1] (**34**)

5. What did the first servant owe? What did the second servant owe? (**24, 28**)

   a. What is your reaction to the differences?

   b. In the original Greek, the first man owed ten thousand talents (one talent was worth about 20 years of wages). The second man owed a hundred denarii (a denarius was the usual daily wage of a day laborer).
      i. Remember, this was a parable about sin and forgiveness. When you think about the enormity of what the first man owed, what do you learn about your own sin?

      ii. About God's grace?

      iii. Write a prayer of gratitude to God.

---

[1] A person lending money could seize the borrower who couldn't pay and force him or his family to work until the debt was paid. The debtor could also be thrown into prison... It was hoped that the debtor, while in prison, would sell off his landholdings or that relatives would pay the debt. If not, the debtor could remain in prison for life. Osborne, Grant, and Philip W. Comfort. *Life Application Bible Commentary Matthew*. Wheaton, IL: Tyndale, 1995. Print. 364

6. What did Jesus declare would happen if we don't forgive our brothers and sisters as we have been forgiven (**35**)? Process this grave warning.

a. Reflect on this quote:

"Because God has forgiven all our sins, we should not withhold forgiveness from others. As we realize how completely Christ has forgiven us, it should produce an attitude of forgiveness towards others. When we don't forgive others, we are setting ourselves above God's law of love."[1]

i. What is your reaction to this quote?

ii. What is God's law of love (**Matthew 22:37–39**)? How is it relevant to forgiveness?

b. Forgiveness is so important to Jesus that He put it in His instructions on how to pray. Read **Matthew 6:9–15** and comment on the importance of forgiveness.

⁹ Pray like this: Our Father in heaven, may your name be kept holy. ¹⁰ May your Kingdom come soon. May your will be done on earth, as it is in heaven. ¹¹ Give us today the food we need, ¹² and forgive us our sins, as we have forgiven those who sin against us.

¹³ And don't let us yield to temptation, but rescue us from the evil one. ¹⁴ "If you forgive those who sin against you, your heavenly Father will forgive you. ¹⁵ But if you refuse to forgive others, your Father will not forgive your sins.

---

[1] *Life Application Study Bible: New Living Translation*, Carol Stream, IL: Tyndale House, 2014. 1581

c. How does **Ephesians 4:30–32** challenge you about forgiveness?

> *30 And do not bring sorrow to God's Holy Spirit by the way you live. 31 Get rid of all bitterness, rage, anger, harsh words, and slander, as well as all types of evil behavior. 32 Instead, be kind to each other, tenderhearted, forgiving one another, just as God through Christ has forgiven you.*

d. How do you reconcile the above Scriptures with the truth of **Ephesians 2:8–9**?

7. How might/could forgiveness bring freedom to a person's life? To your life?

a. Forgiveness doesn't always mean a restoration of relationship. It means you are no longer imprisoned by hostility toward someone. Think about a person in your life you struggle to forgive. How does this thought help you approach forgiving them?

b. Read through the following Scriptures and underline ways to live a life marked by forgiveness. Discuss them with your group.
   i. **Ephesians 5:1–2**

   > *1 Imitate God, therefore, in everything you do, because you are his dear children. 2 Live a life filled with love, following the example of Christ. He loved us and offered himself as a sacrifice for us, a pleasing aroma to God.*

ii. **Colossians 3:12–15**

¹² Since God chose you to be the holy people he loves, you must clothe yourselves with tenderhearted mercy, kindness, humility, gentleness, and patience. ¹³ Make allowance for each other's faults, and forgive anyone who offends you. Remember, the Lord forgave you, so you must forgive others. ¹⁴ Above all, clothe yourselves with love, which binds us all together in perfect harmony. ¹⁵ And let the peace that comes from Christ rule in your hearts. For as members of one body you are called to live in peace. And always be thankful.

As you do life this week, consider writing out **Colossians 3:12–15** on a note card or Post-it note. Remind yourself each day why you are called to love others and the ways in which you can do it.

Expand Your Understanding

1. After doing this lesson, what new or fresh thought (or thoughts) do you have about Jesus?

2. In light of this new or fresh thought (or thoughts), how would you describe Him to a friend?

3. How will this new or fresh thinking about Jesus affect your everyday life?

Prayer Requests

GRACE ENCOUNTERS
Lesson 7
Acts 8:26–40

Experience the Story

Before you start answering this week's questions, slowly read **Acts 8:26–40**. Read it as you've never read it before. Imagine you're part of the story. What do you see? Hear? Feel? Do you see yourself in the story? Let the passage come alive for you, and then talk to God about what you noticed.

26 As for Philip, an angel of the Lord said to him, "Go south down the desert road that runs from Jerusalem to Gaza." 27 So he started out, and he met the treasurer of Ethiopia, a eunuch of great authority under the Kandake, the queen of Ethiopia. The eunuch had gone to Jerusalem to worship, 28 and he was now returning. Seated in his carriage, he was reading aloud from the book of the prophet Isaiah.

29 The Holy Spirit said to Philip, "Go over and walk along beside the carriage." 30 Philip ran over and heard the man reading from the prophet Isaiah. Philip asked, "Do you understand what you are reading?"

31 The man replied, "How can I, unless someone instructs me?" And he urged Philip to come up into the carriage and sit with him. 32 The passage of Scripture he had been reading was this: "He was led like a sheep to the slaughter. And as a lamb is silent before the shearers, he did not open his mouth. 33 He was humiliated and received no justice. Who can speak of his descendants? For his life was taken from the earth."

34 The eunuch asked Philip, "Tell me, was the prophet talking about himself or someone else?" 35 So beginning with this same Scripture, Philip told him the Good News about Jesus.

36 As they rode along, they came to some water, and the eunuch said, "Look! There's some water! Why can't I be baptized?" 38 He ordered the carriage to stop, and they went down into the water, and Philip baptized him.

39 When they came up out of the water, the Spirit of the Lord snatched Philip away. The eunuch never saw him again but went on his way rejoicing. 40 Meanwhile, Philip found himself farther north at the town of Azotus. He preached the Good News there and in every town along the way until he came to Caesarea.

_____

_____

_____

_____

_____

_____

_____

Background

After the resurrection and ascension of Jesus, believers waited as He had asked them to do. Sure enough, Holy Spirit came (Acts 2). The Spirit of God poured Himself out on believers and they began to share the story of Jesus wherever they went. Three thousand people responded to Peter's powerful sermon and received salvation in one day! Miraculous signs and wonders were being performed. Then, great opposition rose up against this newly-empowered movement of Christ followers. Stephen was arrested based on false testimony and in response to the accusations gave an articulate recounting of the story of God's plan through Jesus. Jewish leaders were infuriated. Acts 7 tells the tragic story of how Stephen became the first Christian martyr.

The beginning of Acts 8 follows the stoning of Stephen this way: "A great wave of persecution began that day, sweeping over the church in Jerusalem; and all the believers except the apostles were scattered through the regions of Judea and Samaria." The persecuted believers preached the good news about Jesus wherever they went. At this point a man named Philip[1] became one of the first to preach the gospel outside of Jerusalem. He went first to Samaria.[2] Crowds there listened to him because they were eager to hear his message and see the miracles he performed. This lesson traces Philip's steps out of public ministry in Samaria and in to personal evangelism on a desert road. **Acts 8:26–40** shows us that each of his steps was orchestrated by God in order to reach one particular man.

---

[1] This is not the apostle Philip (see **John 1:43, 44**) but a Greek-speaking Jew, "full of the Spirit and wisdom" (**Acts 6:3**), who was one of the seven men chosen to help with the food distribution program in the church. (**Acts 6:5**)

[2] The Samaritans were considered half-breeds by the "pure" Jews in the southern kingdom of Judah, and the two groups hated each other intensely. But Jesus Himself went into Samaria (**John 4**), and He commanded His followers to spread the Good News there. (**Acts 1:8**)

The Big Idea

Have you or someone you know ever wound up in a unique or difficult situation, only to conclude that God was behind it, orchestrating circumstances in order to spread the gospel? Perhaps a family relocated due to an unexpected job transfer and wound up sharing Christ with new neighbors. Or perhaps a person received a cancer diagnosis and later discovered how God used them to encourage others each time they went for chemotherapy. When we study Scripture and when we pay close attention in our own lives, we find that God uses subtle and obvious promptings in order to position a person at the right place at the right time. As a result they can share Christ with someone God has prepared to hear about Him. That's what we discover in this lesson when Philip followed God amidst persecution.

Dig In

1. Read **Acts 8:1–5** to get a better sense of what was going on after the death of Stephen.[1] In this situation, what impact did persecution of the believers seem to have on reaching the lost?

   a. Think about what it might have been like for those who were persecuted and scattered. Describe what comes to mind.

   b. What role, if any, do you think obedience to God played in their lives at this point?

---

[1] Persecution pushed the Christians beyond Jerusalem and into Judea and Samaria, thus fulfilling the second part of Jesus' command (see **Acts 1:8**). The persecution helped spread the Good News. God would bring great results from the believers' suffering. *Life Application Study Bible: New Living Translation*, Carol Stream, IL: Tyndale House, 2014.

2. According to **Acts 8:6**, why did the crowds in Samaria listen so intently to Philip?

Read **verses 7**, **8** and **12** and comment on the impact of Philip's ministry.

3. In **Acts 8:26–28**, things took a sudden turn for Philip. Who spoke to Philip to give him his next instructions?

   a. How did Philip respond and what happened next?

   b. What do you learn from **verses 27** and **28** about the man Philip met?[1]

4. Read **Acts 8:29–31**. Who spoke to Philip to give him instructions next?

   a. Describe how Philip responded to the Holy Spirit.

---

[1] We do not know much about Philip's background. But we know enough of the Ethiopian that he was very different from the Christian Jew, Philip. He was probably a black-skinned African of a high standing who had servants attending to him as he traveled in his chariot.

b. Read through the following verses. Underline two key words or phrases about the Holy Spirit and note how it impacts you.

   i. **John 14:15–16**

   If you love Me, obey My commandments. And I will ask the Father, and He will give you another Advocate, who will never leave you.

   ii. **John 14:26**

   But when the Father sends the Advocate as my representative— that is the Holy Spirit—He will teach you everything and will remind you of everything I have told you.

   iii. **John 16:7–8**

   ⁷ But in fact, it is best for you that I go away, because if I don't the Advocate won't come. If I do go away, then I will send Him to you. ⁸ And when He comes, He will convict the world of its sin, and of God's righteousness, and of the coming judgment.

   iv. **Romans 8:26–27**

   ²⁶ And the Holy Spirit helps us in our weakness. For example, we don't know what God wants us to pray for. But the Holy Spirit prays for us with groanings that cannot be expressed in words. ²⁷ And the Father who knows all hearts knows what the Spirit is saying, for the Spirit pleads for us believers in harmony with God's own will.

c. From **Acts 8:30–31**, what do you notice about Philip's spiritual conversation with the Ethiopian man?

d. How would you describe the Ethiopian man's response to Philip? (**8:31**)

5. Read **Acts 8:32–35**.[1] Philip used the man's question as the starting point to explain the good news of Jesus. Can you describe a time when someone's question allowed you to explain more about Jesus to them? Was it a biblical question? A question about a life issue? Something else?

Talk with your group about how you bridged the person's question to Jesus, or how you wish you would have known how to do that.

6. Philip's spiritual conversation was especially interesting because spiritual rejection of eunuchs and foreigners by Jews[2] was commonplace in that day. What does this say to you about Philip?

7. Read the following quote.
"Philip discovered that the Ethiopian had been prepared by God before he even spoke to him. We too can expect this as we share Christ with others. As we share, we are often surprised to find that the person with whom we are talking has been prepared by God for the encounter. This doesn't always happen, of course, but happens often enough for us to realize that God can lead us to people whom he has already prepared to listen to what we have to say. We are just one link in what God is doing in that person's life."[3]

---

[1] The Ethiopian was reading from **Isaiah 53:7–8**
[2] **Isaiah 56:3–8**
[3] Fernando, Ajith. *The NIV Application Commentary: ACTS*. Zondervan, 1998.

a. How does the quote encourage you to talk to people about Jesus?

b. Have you ever experienced something like this in your own life? If so, process it with your group.

8. Read **Acts 8:36–40**. What resulted from the conversation between Philip and the Ethiopian man?

a. How might the man have known to ask about baptism?

b. List some of the reasons you think this man had to rejoice.

c. From **verses 39–40,** note your concluding thoughts about Philip. What strikes you about his character, life and ministry?

Expand Your Understanding

1. After doing this lesson, what new or fresh thought (or thoughts) do you have about Jesus?

2. In light of this new or fresh thought (or thoughts), how would you describe Him to a friend?

3. How will this new or fresh thinking about Jesus affect your everyday life?

Prayer Requests